Rule Britannia Books

Presents…

"Mummy Says…
Daddy Says"

A selection of quotes and revealing statements from children about their parents interspersed with a few choice quotes from seasoned parents about their beloved offspring

By
Jules Ede

Matador
9 Priory Business Park,
Wistow Road, Kibworth Beauchamp,
Leicestershire. LE8 0RX
Tel: 0116 279 2299
Email: books@troubador.co.uk
Web: www.troubador.co.uk/matador
Twitter: @matadorbooks

ISBN 978 1788037 792

British Library Cataloguing in Publication Data.
A catalogue record for this book is available from the British Library.

Printed and bound by CPI Group (UK) Ltd, Croydon, CR0 4YY
Typeset in Stroudley 16pt by Troubador Publishing Ltd, Leicester, UK

Matador is an imprint of Troubador Publishing Ltd

Illustrations
by
Mike Lacey

Through
The Beehive Illustration Agency
Cirencester
GLOS

CONTENTS

PREFACE

Having been fortunate enough to have lived on the affluent border of South-west London and Surrey for the past fourteen years, I have had the opportunity to observe and analyse family life of some of it's comfortable residents and their privileged children from several different aspects.

I felt that it was perhaps an appropriate time for me to attempt to sketch an authentic but affectionate caricature of some of these parents and children, by using a canvas of some scenarios and situations that they might be experiencing in their everyday lives.

Stencilled sparingly between some of these portraits are a few choice quotations from children about their parents and some parental quotes about their beloved offspring that I hope you might also find entertaining.

DEDICATION

This book is dedicated to the many parents
who might be struggling with many issues
as they attempt to guide their beloved offspring
up to, and eventually through the challenging
years of adolescence.

SCHOOL CHOICE

Daddy says it's important to be able to make friends with everyone in my class at school.

It will enable me to mix with, share and appreciate the many facets of the rich cultural and ethnic diversity that exist in current British society, equipping me with the skills and abilities to become a tolerant and compassionate member of our inclusive nation.

I attend St Andrew's Private School for Young Ladies and have already made a lot of really cool chums while playing Lacrosse, during fencing practice and at our pony club dressage classes.

FACES

The innocent face of a child can say a thousand words…

If you can manage to stop the mouth parts moving for a minute.

SHARING

There are three things that children are always happy to share…

Nasal mucus secretions;
Animal poo deposits on their shoes.
The precise age of their parents.

THE GENE POOL

As he looked into the little squinting eyes opposite him, watching the podgy little wrinkled face, the bald head with scaly scalp, the plump little open hands, and the pouting lips, making strange gurgling sounds...

Little Freddie had to accept...

The life guard at the gene pool was definitely off duty the day that he was conceived!...

RECIPROCATION

Mummy says...

A father teaches his son about the important things in life such as football, carpentry, the action and function of a ball cock, the importance of surface preparation prior to painting, and the correct protocol to be followed when sharpening garden tools.

In return a son teaches his father... how to reprogramme the remote control... yet again.

THE NURSERY

Mummy said when my brothers and sisters were young and became over excited and totally out of control, she would have no option but to use the nursery… then bolt the door.

It wasn't until Daddy came home in the evening that he was finally able to persuade her to leave it.

THE ZOO

After weeks of repeated requests, my daddy has finally agreed to take me to the zoo next week.

Mummy says that if they really wanted me that much, they would have made their own collection, confinement, quarantine and transportation arrangements.

PEACE

What do you call a place where

1. The noise of whining children is never heard.

2. A vigorous massage to your spinal vertebrae is available only as a requested optional extra.

3. You are able to enjoy the whole contents of your drink, without fear of sharing half of it over your, or your neighbour's lap.

Answer… " First Class Section"

FOUR-WHEEL DRIVE

Mummy says we have to have a four-wheel drive SUV as it allows us to go off-road whenever we desire, to fully explore and appreciate the benefits of our beautiful countryside.

The elevated driving position gives us a commanding view of the road and permits us to drive through fords and across flowing streams with total confidence and the four wheel drive traction in deep snow during the winter months is a real godsend.

We reside in Knightsbridge, within the Borough of Kensington and Chelsea, Central London.

SLEEPOVERS

Mummy says if I'm asking school friends over for a sleepover, I can only invite the ones who are really polite and refined, respectful and well behaved.

The next day at school I told my friends… "Sorry… but my mummy doesn't do sleepovers."

CARS

Rupert said that his daddy owns a family estate in Berkshire that would take him all day to drive around.

I said I know the feeling…

My dad used to have an old car like that too, but finally traded it in for a more modern one that was much more reliable.

LOFTS

Sebastian at school told me his daddy was so successful he owned three cars and a loft in a rather fashionable part of the old city.

I told him what a strange coincidence, but in a different kind of way…

My dad was unemployed, was not successful, owned three bicycles , and also had a loft , but his contained several parts of a rather unfashionable old settee…

A PRIME SPECIMEN

My daddy proudly boasts that his waist measurement is exactly the same as it was when he was 25 years old and in his prime.

I asked him why he wore his belt at an angle of 45 degrees, and why he had pockets that were so tight they no longer served any purpose.

He said one day he would explain to me, but at the moment I was just too young to understand the concepts of the '80s Asymmetric Fashion movement, and the bio nutritional and holistic benefits of naturally fermented hop products…

JUST LIKE FRUIT

My grandad says, "Children are just like
fruit…
They are at their sweetest just before they
turn bad…"

*Terri Guillemets

COMMUNICATION

It is a fallacy that most modern-day
parents appear to have a problem
communicating positively with their
fractious or unresponsive teenage
children.

If their mobile's engaged…
just send them a text.

HUMAN RIGHTS

Physical assualt, intimidation, coercion, moral corruption, personal injury and verbal abuse are all issues any responsible parent tries to protect their children from.

Until we bring them down to the local Soft Play Centre for the first time…

ORIGINS

"Mummy," I asked Daddy, "where do I come from?" and he went very quiet, then looked quite nervous and then he gave me a long lecture, drawing lots of diagrams and pictures of people's naughty parts.

I only asked because Isabelle in my class said she came from Eastbourne.

CELEBRITY CULTURE

Mummy says as I'm so into 'celebrity fashion culture', she's going to buy me an expensive designer top made from responsibly sourced organic hand-spun Peruvian cotton.

Mummy saw one yesterday in a boutique that she thought I would love, with a single shoulder strap, heavily distressed with frayed seams and designer lacerations front and back, with an inscription that read 'Born Green', by a new designer called Justbene Dunn on his newly launched Naive Label.

Mummy said according to his biog., he used to be a tea towel manufacturer twelve months ago before he had a major equipment malfunction.

BREAKFAST

Mummy says we need to eat a good nutritious breakfast every day.

Our muesli helps to release it's energy slowly to our bodies throughout the day, while our organic smoothies have so many free radicals they help to mop up the accumulated toxins produced by our adolescent metabolisms.

We definitely don't want to emulate the McDonald family at number 46, whose children I've heard obtain their five-a-day from a bar of Cadbury's fruit and nut, a Terry's chocolate orange and a strawberry and black currant individual dessert.

IQ

Daddy says I've got something called a low IQ, which must be quite good as he's going to reward me with the latest Apple laptop.

He says as I seem to spend all my time on Twitter, Instagram and updating my profile on Social network sites, I might as well try to earn some income as something called a Superfluent Lifestyle Blogger, which sounds like a really rewarding and worthwhile career opportunity.

FROM FARM TO FORK

As part of our school's sponsored From Farm to Fork project, parents were asked to help by donating a selection of some basic food samples for their children's class.

Mummy decided to source some of our typical organic items from Waitrose...

Celeriac, Mange tout and Asparagus tips, while the remaining items...

Quale's eggs in aspic, Fromage du Midi and Pate de foie Gras had fortunately just been delivered to our local delicatessen the previous afternoon.

Somehow I don't think mummy quite grasped the full concept of the exercise ...

DEVASTATION

Daddy said when my sister left home for uni a few years ago he and Mum were really devastated, especially when they found out my older brother had rented out her room on Air BnB.

They just couldn't believe he could have done such a thing…
Her room was being advertised at well below the current market rate…

LOVE

They say that the love a child has for their mother or father cannot be quantified…

However, scientific research has shown it does tend to be proportional to the screen resolution of their parent's latest mobile phone…

DRIVING

Daddy says he's a very good driver and extremely skilful at controlling his vehicle.

Mummy says all the scratches on the car happened when Daddy was driving.

Daddy says he passed his driving test first time but Mummy had to take hers twice.

Mummy says Daddy has had several accidents and endorsements for speeding.

Daddy often screeches his tyres as he pulls away at traffic junctions.

Mummy has never been involved in an accident and frequently gives way to other drivers just to make them feel good.

Mummy says her car insurance is half the cost of Daddy's.

Daddy says nothing.

GENERATION GAP

Mummy said it was her duty to teach me many important things to prepare me for the challenges I am going to have to face in life.

Knowledge and skills that her mother had passed onto her, such as cookery, sewing, home economics, child health and welfare, motherhood and sustaining a long-term relationship.

"No sweat," I said, "I had those subjects fully covered…"

"I had already downloaded the relevant apps yesterday when I was waiting for one of my nails to dry…"

TEENAGE BRAINS

My dad told me that children's brains were like little sponges when it came to absorbing information.

Apparently, they can cope with learning five languages at the same time.

My teenage brother Marcus is a good example.

Unfortunately his brain was prematurely saturated with Pokemon, Nintendo and Minecraft, but on the few occasions he does communicate, he appears quite fluent in urban uncouth, Disjointed dialogue, Abbreviated texting and Adolescent articulation.

THE SOUND OF CHILDREN

When you hear the noise of children playing happily together, that sound is a truly wondrous thing.

When you hear that sound suddenly stop...start looking for your Domestic Insurance claim form...

THEORIES

Before I got married I had six theories on how to bring up children.

Now I have six children and absolutely no theories...

* John Wilmot

SCHOOL UNIFORMS

Mother says the principle of wearing a school uniform is really important in present day society.

The uniform conceals all signs of class, wealth and social status, so students can learn to mix in an environment of fraternity, harmony and equality, which I think is the way it should be in educational establishments.

I fail to understand, however, why I receive such strange glances from the general public, when I take my daily constitutional down to our local artisan coffee house, for my cup of Colombian triple roasted, demi caffeinated, Hillside Blend.

KNOWLEDGE

Knowledge is a wonderful thing that takes us many years of effort to acquire, assimilate and appreciate.

Teenagers of course, are exceptions to this rule.

FOOD FOR THOUGHT

We spend a lot of our time persuading our children to eat up their peas, carrots, potatoes and broccoli.

We then complain when they become teenagers and appear to spend much of their time in a state of vegetative semi consciousness.

DOWNLOADS

My son thinks he knows it all, being brought up during the age of information technology, scientific innovation and development.

Yesterday I saw him trying to read some pages of a book, explaining how he was downloading software directly into his brain without the use of any digital interface system, with the exception of his finger turning the pages, of course.

PROPERTY

Daddy and Mummy say by the time my sister and I finish our education and start working, we'd be lucky enough to get a mortgage for a garden shed.

They've already got planning permission for a basement and attic conversion for their house, which they feel would provide us with our own independent accommodation while substantially increasing our marriage potential.

Also solving both their personal long-term residential care requirements at the same time…

ORGANIC OPTION

Mummy says she prefers to use a small local butcher to source our organic meat products.

Most of the supermarket stuff has been highly processed and is full of nitrates, antibiotics and hormones, and she doesn't want her sons developing breasts before we've even had a chance to knock on the door of puberty.

Unlike my dad, unfortunately, for whom it's a little too late.

THE AU PAIR

Mummy says our Lithuanian au pair nanny is like gold dust.

She dresses us each morning, prepares our breakfast then walks us to school.

She does the cleaning, washing and ironing for the rest of the day until it's time to pick us up from school again.

Since she has been with us for the past couple of years, her vocabulary has really improved, learning a lot of really useful English words , such as . . . Cif, Domestos, Persil, Harpic, Hotpoint and Hoover.

THE COMMUTER

Mummy says she has to wash at least three of Daddy's ties each week.

He is usually so tired when he returns home on the train each evening, he drops off asleep and proceeds to tie-dribble.

She recently heard from a fellow commuter that some of the regulars run an open book on how long the dribble will stretch to, before it severs and goes into free fall, creating a secondary reservoir on the sport's section of his newspaper.

Apparently, unbeknown to him, he has also acquired quite a following on social media . . .

SPEED

Daddy says a family's internet broadband speed is inversely proportional to the velocity at which its children are capable of descending a flight of stairs to respond to a request from their parents to join them for a nutritious meal.

VALUE OF MONEY

The best way to teach your ingenuous children the true value of money, is to borrow some from them... preferably at regular intervals.

ROMANTIC CONNECTION

Daddy says he's really blessed that mummy still likes to romantically hold his arm when they go strolling together.

I hadn't the heart to tell him that Mummy confided in me that since he had his electronic cochlear implant, his titanium bionic elbow joint and his new digital pacemaker fitted, her internet connection on her phone was now really incredible…

THE GRADUATE

Daddy says a graduate of Physics asks the question,

"How do the laws of dynamic motion influence the way in which bodies might move in relation to one another?"

A graduate of Biology might pose the question,

"How do living organisms survive and microscopically interact in terms of reproduction, growth and cellular development?"

A graduate of Philosophy or Media Studies might ask the more pertinent and significant question,

"Do you want large or regular French Fries with your order ?"

MORNING REFLECTION

Mummy says she feels awful when she looks at herself in the mirror first thing in the morning, and sees someone with piggy little eyes and tangled hair.

But then she looks down on the floor and sees Rufus curled up in his favorite blanket, snoring with his stubby little wet nose, deposits of dried food debris around his mouth and in his hair, with a string of copious saliva dribbling from the side of his mouth, replenishing a substantial reservoir already deposited on the bedroom floor.

Suddenly she doesn't feel so bad after all.

Rufus, I'm ashamed to admit...
is the name of my father.

PETS

Mummy says we're not allowed to have pets as they are unhygienic, too time-demanding and would require a lot of attention, grooming and commitment to their long term care.

I guess I'll just have to be contented with Oscar, Algernon and Primrose… my pet headlice.

WISDOM

A wise father is one who raises his child just high enough for them to be able to reach their dreams.

An unwise father is one who raises his child so high, only to discover he has left his groin area totally unprotected…

Mike Lacey
Illustrator

After having left school with an A-Level in art Mike joined Link studios in London.

Soon after he started working on children's Comics – Whizzer and Chips, Shivver and Shake etc. creating a lot of new strips including Sid's Snake, X-Ray Specs, and many more.

After a few years when kid's comics were in decline thanks to computers and smartphones, Mike left Link Studios to join another agency that was unfortunately starting to specialise in other fields that he had less interest in.

On the advice of a friend Mike decided to join The Beehive Illustration Agency, with whom he has now been with for the past eleven years.

Additional copies of this book are available
online from the Book shop at

www.troubador.co.uk